JUDY SHIMEK DRECHSLER

FALLING INTO *One*

Publishing-Partners

Publishing-Partners
Marcia Breece
Port Townsend, WA 98368
www.Publishing-Partners.com

Copyright © 2016 by Judy Drechsler

All rights reserved. No part of this book may be reproduced, stored in, or introduced into a retrieval system, or transmitted in any form, or by any means (electronic, mechanical, photocopying, recording, or otherwise) without the prior written permission of the publisher.

Printed in the United States of America

Library of Congress Control Number: 2016956205

ISBN: 978-1-944887-15-5

Cover design: Jane Jessen

*right: Yosemite Waterfall
by Frederick Ferdinand Schafer*

For Jakob, James and Wyatt Jo

Table of Contents

Published Poetry and Readings | vii
Foreword | ix
Meditation on Shunryū Suzuki's Waterfall | xi

Section One: Toward the Precipice | 1
    Beach Walk Musings | 3
    Two Haiku ater Beach Walk | 4
    The Seagull | 5
    New River Junction | 6
    Class Reunion | 7
    Bubi's Lamp | 8
    Morning Breaks with Hope | 9
    The Present Moment after Rumi | 10

Section Two: Separate Lives | 11
    The Garden in Winter | 13
    Hands | 14
    After School at 10 | 15
    The Child Gazes Upward | 16
    When I Am 8 | 18
    Mother Shimek | 19
    At Ellis Pond | 20
    I Sit Alone | 22
    The Spider with a Round Back End That Would Make Any Kardashian Jealous | 23
    Waiting For Asparagus | 24
    Spring | 25
    Lady Bug, Lady Bug, Fly Away Home | 26

Section Three: Rays of Sunlight | 27
    Reflection | 29
    The Open Road | 30
    Blue Highways | 31
    500 Miles | 32
    Driving Over the Cascades | 34
    Burg Elts Castle | 35
    Ginger | 36
    Istanbul, the Third Afternoon | 38
    Twelve Women of Istanbul | 39
    Istanbul Impressions in Six Movements | 40

Section Four: Return into One | 43
    In the Redwood Grove, Spreading Ashes | 45
    Old Growth | 46
    Fire in the Bitterroot Valley | 48
    Just Add Water | 49
    Ypres | 50
    I Stand in Front of a Vacant Lot Overgrown Grass and Weeds Waving Back and Forth | 52
    When God Says No | 54
    Alone | 55
    When I Look at My Mother | 56
    A Walk on Pebble Beach | 57
    I Was There to Hear Your Last Breath | 58
    About the Author | 61
    Gratitude | 63

Published Poetry and Readings

Judy Shimek Drechsler

2010
    Beach Walk Musings | page 3
    Shape of Water juried show/Maritime Center
    Port Townsend, WA

2014
    Northwind Arts Center
    30 Minute Reading 5/22/14
    Port Townsend, WA

    The Voyage
    Polaris K-12 20-Year Anniversary Program 9/12/14
    Anchorage, AK

2015
    Gallery Showing
    First Presbyterian Church January/February/2015
    Port Townsend, WA

    ARS Poetica
    Juried Art/Poetry
    "where art and poetry meet" 3 poems

    The Garden in Winter | page 13
    Margaret Gibbs oil paints

    Blue Highways | page 31
    Merle Jones oil paints
    Displayed at Collective Visions Gallery May 2015
    Reading 5/24/15

    A Walk on Pebble Beach | page 57
    Jamie Dample oil paints
    Displayed at Isella Salon Spa, Bremerton, WA
    May 2015
    and Poulsbohemian Coffee House July 2015,
    Reading 7/11/15

2016
    ARS Poetica
    Juried Art/Poetry Show
    "where art and poetry meet" 3 poems

    When God Says No | page 54
    Abel oil paints

    Reflection | page 29
    Erin Pocuis oil paints
    Displayed at Toro Lounge, Bremerton, WA
    May 2015
    Reading 5/24/15

    Waiting For Asparagus | page 24
    Elaine Greene Mosaics
    Displayed at Front Street Gallery
    Reading 4/17/16

    Ladybug, Ladybug, Fly Away Home | page 26
    YOUR DAILY POEM
    Online Poetry 3/19/2016

    The Spider with a Round Back End
    That Would Make Any
    Kardashian Jealous | page 23
    Rainshadow Poetry Anthology 2016
    Reading 5/1/16

Foreword

I first heard of Shunryū Suzuki when I watched the movie, "The Wisdom of Parrots." An analogy Suzuki made intrigued me, and I bought his book to read about it.

In *Zen Mind, Beginner's Mind*, Suzuki tells a story about a trip to Yosemite. While there, he stopped to watch one of the many huge waterfalls. He likened it to a curtain thrown from the top of a mountain, spreading out into many streams and individual droplets. Each drop appeared to come down extremely slowly because of the distance. The water remained separate drops until it reached the bottom. There, the individual droplets came back together into one stream.

My poem, "Meditation on Suzuki-Roshi's Waterfall," from which the name of this book of poems is taken, came from this analogy. All living beings, he says, including animals and plants, are part of one great body of water. When the water reaches the cliff, which is life, it breaks up into many individual living things, all experiencing their lives until they arrive at the bottom and become one river again.

I first experienced the waterfalls of Yosemite on a trip there with my son, Jo, who later died of cancer, so waterfalls have taken on a special meaning for me.

— *Judy Drechsler, November 2016*

MEDITATION ON SHUNRYŪ SUZUKI'S WATERFALL
2010

Water flows to the precipice,
seeks the ground.
One drop falls,
then another,
separating into separate lives.
Through the rainbow of mist and shower,
rays of sunlight travel with it.
Drops come together,
return into one.

left: Yosemite Waterfall
by Frederick Ferdinand Schafer
oil – 23 x 16

section one
TOWARD THE PRECIPICE

BEACH WALK MUSINGS
2010

Water takes the shape
  of its container
  flows down paths
  of least resistance

The sea sloshes
  around in a
  big bowl
  escaping when
  it can onto dryness

Where it reaches
  for treasure
  to pull
  into the depths

And takes what it can
  on a journey
  smoothing
  many edges

Exhibited in **Shape of Water**, *an exhibition of visual art and poetry. Presented by the Port Townsend Arts Commission and the Northwest Maritime Center, April 10 – June 30, 2010*

Left page: "Little Chiton" by Mare Tietjen

Two Haiku After Beach Walk
2010

footprints on damp sand
waves sweep them into the sea
fleeting memory

waves play with my toes
chase my footprints on the sand
rollick, frolic, gone

The Seagull
2010

keeps pace

with the

ferry

one on

white capped

waves;

one on

a single

shaft of air,

swooping

gracefully

up and down

like a child

on a slide.

New River Junction
2010

Still at last
standing on the steep bank,
river flowing past like
the moving walkway at
the airport.
I want to step out onto it
and see where it takes me.

Dark and green with soil and plants
stripped from its flanks
constantly increasing its breadth
inch by inch.
Trees creep toward the edge
as close as they can
without slipping into
the wet, muddy life source,
relentlessly seeking the ocean.

The water swallows the sky,
meanders, wanders,
creating curves and loops,
ignoring the creations of man,
sometimes making them
a passenger
on an unwanted journey.

A formidable power
despite its soothing appearance.

Class Reunion
2010

The road home
beckons,
like an old lover
whose face lies
half hidden
within the far
reaches of
your mind.

Like a thin worn
ribbon
the road retreats
in twists and turns
calling to us from
past lives,
come home once more,
come home.

Bubi's Lamp
2011

It sits on my
kitchen counter
recalling memories

of being perched
on a narrow shelf
at the top of the stairs

matches lying ready
to help light the way
into the aromatic darkness

my small feet
negotiate wooden steps
into the night time

of the root cellar
dried apples, yellow pears
red cherries piled high

small cucumbers pickled
in crocks
floating in dill

potatoes waiting
to be mashed
on a cold winter's day

canned tomatoes and beans
longing for the soup pot
winter survival resides here

Morning Breaks With Hope
2009

Morning breaks with hope, the body a perfect shell, like the rising sun, life dawns bright and fresh, a child grows swiftly in cool delicate breezes, nurtured by balmy rays, snug in the rich soil of family, cradled in grass, glistening with dew.

Noontide, life's meridian, filled with job and family, and then children who create mornings of their own, heat and happiness ride the swiftly moving clouds towards sunset.

Evening knocks on the door, slanting sunrays settle on our shoulders, streaks of pink slice the gray edges of life, stars are jewels left behind for loved ones, as sunset fades to black.

THE PRESENT MOMENT AFTER RUMI
2015

when you contemplate lines on a leaf,
    wings on a butterfly
a moment is born
    cradled in the arms of the present
complete in its isolation
    suspended in a wall of time

assaulted by the haggard crone calling you
back to
    past events, broken dreams

while Ulysses' sirens call you forward
    Encouraging you to scan the
horizon
    to dream of future possibilities

shed these unwanted companions
so each moment can be *conscious of itself*
or you miss the garden

section two
SEPARATE LIVES

The Garden in Winter
2014

Coffee and pears
in a sunny window,
gazing out at
crumpled hills
of brown dirt
embraced in the grip
of red clover to
provide nutrients for
spring planting.

The garden lives
in winter death,
soil in disarray
from the unearthing
of potatoes,
brown stalks
stick up,
colorful flowers
just a memory.

Lettuce and spinach
bolted to seed
now chicken feed,
only asparagus fronds
and garlic bulbs,
not quite done,
wave with
frantic life
in the winter winds.

Left: Garden in Winter by Margarete Gibbs
fabric - 12 x 15

HANDS
2015

We're standing in my son's kitchen
drying dishes,
sun streaming in
through bright California morning.
Your fingers are so short,
my son says.

Startled, I hold my hand out to look.
Well, yes, compared to his fingers and
my daughter's long piano-playing digits
they do seem on the short side.

I don't know why this dismays me.
Is it because my children are not
mirror images of me after all?
Or that short fingers are
not appealing to me, when my
image of them was long and slender?

As I look at them now,
they show signs of life.
They changed diapers,
set the table,
rolled out pie dough,
scrubbed the floor,
hung sheets in the
warm afternoon to dry,
caressed the cheeks of
my children,
closed my son's eyes
as he died,
cradled my grandsons'
fuzzy, soft, baby heads.

After School at 10
2015

I open my parents' bedroom door, the faint
creak it always makes loud now in the empty
house, the sun casting a shadowy film over the
dresser that holds my mother's jewelry box.
I make my way across the room to slowly open
the black box with roses carved on its lid.

My mother's jewels brighten the room as if in
a spotlight, soon earrings large as the white
daisies in our yard cover my ears, a necklace
of pearls, real I'm sure, will reach to my waist
so I wrap it around my neck twice and hold a
sparkly blue broach to my Red Ryder sweat
shirt.

The "diamond" bracelet slips onto my tiny wrist
and stays on only if I keep my arm extended
upward the better to admire its elegance.

Rings of all hues slide around my small fingers
sparkling in the late afternoon sunshine.

I am beautiful

The Child Gazes Upward
2014

Silver chains hold her
steady
in the wooden swing
make of her
a gentle pendulum
on the front porch
shaded by branches
of giant maples
and oaks reaching out.

Off the swing quickly
when great-grandmother
calls her to come in
for a snack.
She runs
through the living room
past the large radio
in its curved, polished cabinet,
hears the mid-1940s
voices call out the news.

Glances at the black
wooden window seat,
knows that when she raises
the lid, there will be candy
if she is good, one for her
mouth right away,
one for her pocket.

Bubbles float
at the top
of a tall glass of milk
next to a
flaky round
kolache
filled with bright
cherries from the tree
outside the window.

If it were spring
eggs would be sitting
safely in a basket
next to the warm stove,
carefully covered,
until new chicks
pecked their way out.

She hurries in to find a seat
at the square kitchen table
with a spooner, sugar shaker,
salt and pepper
in the middle,
clean white cloth napkin
covering them to keep
off flies and dust.

When I Am 8

2011

The pincers navigate
frantically across
my knuckles,
up and down my arm,
searching for the
cool water from
which they were
recently plucked.

Squatted onto
my heels I sit
at the edge of the
sluggish creek,
my feet
soaking up
sandy wetness
underneath.

The crawdad makes his frenzied trek
across my skin.
The underbelly of the
old stone bridge
rises dark and dank
above me.

I am 8 years old.

MOTHER SHIMEK
2013

I see her through
the screen door:
gray dress
sensible black shoes
brown tweed coat
short white hair
covered with a hairnet
wire framed glasses
shopping bag over her arm.

A quiet woman
my Grandmother
beaten down by life
abusive father
and husband
too many kids
seven boys, one girl
a life of
hard work
and poverty.

She raises a hand
as she walks by
never stops to talk
there is no memory
in my mind
of her voice
only the tart
taste of the dill
pickles she made
every year.

At Ellis Pond
For My Father
2010

Tiny hills and valleys of water pushed by the wind slide across Ellis Pond.

Nearly a century ago a small boy, dirty bare feet digging into the earth, perches at the top of the hill. He watches the big machines push black dirt ever higher as the Ellis Golf Course takes shape. Soon he runs errands for the workmen and gathers pennies for lost balls buried in the muddy water and bushes that surround the pond. Cash is important to a boy who has the toes cut out of his shoes to make them fit.

He is 15 when his father deserts the family, 6 brothers and a sister. He quits school and goes to work at the Quaker Oats Company. The passion that saves him is sports. An emotional outlet and wild success at whatever he tries, diving, swimming, tennis, wrestling, golf. Strong, and loving competition, he excels at speed skating, becoming a member of the 1939 Olympic Speed Skating team. He is known for his beautiful Olympic stroke. Instead World War II starts and he flies gliders and bombers.

After the war, he sells Schilling Spices and Buicks, does police work. At 45, he is back at Ellis Golf Course, where he is known as the Paul Bunyan of golf, a long ball hitter. For 25 years he is head Golf Pro and a beloved teacher to young and old learning to play. Today a memorial bench dedicated to him sits by the 9th green near the water where tiny hills and valleys of water pushed by the wind slide across Ellis Pond.

I Sit Alone
1984

I sit alone
in a shabby Alaskan diner
scratched tables
mismatched chairs

sun rays bouncing off icicles
hanging from the roof
time alone
to think

newly divorced

hot coffee, gray clouds of steam
floating above

frosted cinnamon roll,
warm and sweet
comfort food

fried egg, over easy
cigarette smoke curling upward
newspaper open

recovering myself
after 22 years of being

someone else

The spider with a round back end that would make any Kardashian jealous
2015

creates a dinner table of diaphanous
strings capable of holding a cornucopia
of sustenance, stored in silk cupboards,
a juicy black fly, a powdery moth.

She hides at the edge of the web
in the daytime to avoid becoming
dinner herself for the birds,
who also grocery shop every day,

or avoids predators by
appearing to be
inedible or unappetizing
like Aunt Anne's oyster dressing.

Should the wind or human carelessness
destroy or damage, she recreates
the floating restaurant
uncoiling the silent string

birthed from her spinnerets
to set the table invitingly
for the next unwilling
guest that knocks on the door.

WAITING FOR ASPARAGUS
2014

Two years ago I dug
a twelve-inch ditch to hold
the crowns, pushed them down
into fertile black soil,
covered them with dirt
so darkness could encourage creativity.

The ditch disappeared
became smooth dark soil
green tips poked up,
seeking sunlight and air.

Three years, they told me,
before my mouth could
close down over
green spears,
savor their goodness,
roasted, steamed,
or eaten raw with salt.

Yet they rise up
taller than I am,
dancing in the wind,
a fan cooling the sun's brow,
red tinted berries hanging
delicately from some.

Yellow butterflies with white dots
on their top wings hover
over feathery fronds
which shed their vanity,
turning brown
in fall chill.

Spring

2013

clutching my neck scarf
closer around my face
to cheat the cold
assulting my nose

head down
feet quickly moving
towards home and
my warm living room

cursing the icy
January wind
I glance up
and see

delicate pink petals
defying the sting
of the
winter wind

no neck scarf to
protect against
frost sure to
arrive soon

a messenger of
warmer days
and juicy fruit
to come

Lady Bug, Lady Bug, Fly Away Home
2011

A lady bug
has been living
in my bathroom
since August,
watching me bathe
and brush my teeth.

"Hello," I say
each morning.
All winter she sat
clinging to ceiling or wall.
"What are you eating?"
I'd ask.

I'd carefully take her
into my hand
and place her gently
on the spiderplant leaf
hoping she would
find sustenance.

Now she
has disappeared.
The ceiling is
empty again.
I hope she isn't dead;
Spring is nearly here.

section three
RAYS OF SUNLIGHT

REFLECTION
2009

the lake is quiet
in the early morning,
still and shimmering

the slanting rays
of rising sun
reach for the
deep darkness
of the
lake bottom

motorboats
not yet awake
the surface a mirror
of surrounding forest

I paddle the kayak
creating ripples
that flow eternally
outward

only birdsong

murmurs my name

*left: Reflections, by Erin Pocius,
oil – 12 x 24*

The Open Road
2011

Rolling down the rain-soaked highway
awaiting the next turn in the road
that might be anticipated,
but could be unexpected.

Off for a week of adventures,
no schedule,
nowhere to be,
out of cell and internet range,
we fly along unconnected.

Trees rise like the green walls
of a long, curvy tunnel.
My red socks
propped up on the dash
feel the heat of the engine.

Mist perches on top of the
green hills
like peaked, gray hats.
Drops decorate the windshield,
a cemetery for bugs.

Garrison Keillor drones on in a voice
that massages the mind into drowsiness.
Dark, blue-green water
races along in the opposite direction
carving out a road of its own.

Blue Highways
2011

spider lines across the map,
freedom from routine and chores of home
meandering down the back roads
no destination in mind

wind in my face, suntanned arm
out the window,
one hand on the wheel
each bend in the road brings
small slices of life

a farmer tills the field,
sheets flap in the wind
a woman reaches
for more clothespins

she glances up
I pass through with a wave
and a nod
to strangers I will never see again

500 Miles
2011

7 AM early start
cross the Kentucky line
into West Virginia
stray thunderstorms stalk us
possible baseball size hail
heavy rain
high winds
tornadoes possible

Springtime is fix-it season
Road Work One Mile
Fines Double in Work Areas
Right Lane Closed 1500 ft.
Slower Traffic Keep Right
that would be us

We find our way
wandering the back roads
life doesn't happen on the interstate*
77 degrees at 11:06
GPS recalculating
Stay on 79 for 148 miles
then turn left,

Parallel ribbons of concrete
take us into Maryland
Maryland, the Old Line State
Maryland Wild Life
Watch For It Enjoy It
my mind wanders
does Blooming Rose Road
have blooming roses on it?

Trucks loaded with
the staples of our life
roar past us
No Trucks Over 5 Tons
On US 40 Alternate
Truckers Steep Descent 6%
Next 13 Miles
Run Away Truck Ramp
One Mile

Our house on wheels
devouring miles
like a hungry lion
until our bellies
growl in competition
with the
big cat's
empty gut
time for gas

From Blue Highways by William Least Heat-Moon

Driving Over the Cascades
2009

Shades of green
crowding the road
slicing through the
mountains

Ribbon of glacier turquoise
the Skagit hugs one side
racing west
towards Puget Sound

Small islands of rock
dot the river's expanse
stumpy trees valiantly grow
in sparse soil

Civilization intrudes
a small parking lot
overwhelmed
with cars and tourists

Brown signs tell the future
Ross Resort ahead
Lookout, 1800 ft
Slow Vehicle Turnout
25 mph curves

BURG ELTS CASTLE
2012

it should be peopled
with ghosts
knights in chain mail
crossbows and swords ready
ladies in long, flowing dresses
sewing endlessly on dark tapestries

instead there are roads
a white bus zooms along
carrying tourists
to yet another ancient site

a couple on bicycles
peddle their way
to the next small village
he in a white cap
her dark hair flying loose
in the wind

grape vines march up steep hills
in straight lines across
the once forested landscape
a vintner's tiny bulldozer
clinging to the steep hillside
rolls along between the rows

rolling hills of a tamed landscape
rows of tended vines and geometric
fields under the gold and red Metternich
flag flying in the 21st century breeze

Ginger
2014

I watch the seagull perched assertively
on the bow of the boat.
He eyes the neophyte sailors
with beady eyes,
ruffling his feathers in warning
if we get too close.
Ginger, a stout, wooden old lady,
doesn't seem to mind.

Learn the lingo,
starboard, port, hull,
fore, aft,
reef, luff, moor.
Riding the waves
is like joining the military,
short snappy orders
must be instantly obeyed
lest the sails luff,
the boat lose its way
and drift.

Sound is different
on the water,
boards creak, sails shudder,
the clank of
weighing anchor,
the squeaks and groans
as you hoist the sail,
the slap of the waves,
the call of the seagull
puffs of wind that whisper
past your ear and
belly out the sails,

At the helm
I feel the pull of the water,
the horizon a flat line
before me,
the wake of the craft
now a highway for a gull
who follows, using the wind too,
to stay above the waves.

ISTANBUL, THE THIRD AFTERNOON
2012

Tuesday, four p.m. in Turkey,
six a.m. in Washington, USA.
We have been here three days.
Did a load of laundry.
The clothes are still damp.

Mac tries the debit card.
The machine is contrary.
"Your card has been
declined by your bank."
The clothes are still damp.

Must call bank later tonight
when it is ten hours
earlier in Washington, USA.
Then they will want to know
many things to prove it is us.

Last four digits of your social Security number?
What was your first pet's name?
What was your Mother's maiden name?
Where was your first job?
What city were you born in?

I might recall the last one, but
my mind is so stuffed
with new images, smells and impressions,
that the details of my identity elude me.
And the clothes are still damp.

Twelve Women of Istanbul

2015

Twelve women of Istanbul
sit shoulder to shoulder, the vanity of hair

tucked into silky headscarves

with flowers floating in a field of blue,
yellow
swirls, stripes, and
plain beige, an anomaly

among the fashionable.

From serviceable black shoes, white socks
peek out
as one removes a shoe to rest her foot.
Shawls cover plump shoulders.

The women smile, laugh and chat,
hands
folded in their laps, legs crossed
at the ankles, smiling at me demurely.

A blue print dress, one sunny yellow,
another bold red, stripes circling the hem,
one bright sweater to proclaim youth

but mostly long dark coats buttoned to the neck.

The ancient stone wall
in the background
dark and cracked,
full of their history,

obstinately silent

as the call to prayer rings out.

ISTANBUL IMPRESSIONS IN SIX MOVEMENTS
2012

I.
   Hot, toasty brown
   chestnuts, the smell
   of roasted corn
   piled on small carts.
   The disabled and elderly
   offer small packs
   of Kleenex in the hope
   of a coin or two.
   Thin women hold out
   their hands,
   pointing to the children
   they pull along.
   In slivers of space,
   women in head scarves,
   men with dark mustaches,
   hawk jewelry and blue
   glass eyes to ward off evil.
   The crowds flow past,
   often without a glance.
   My feet blister from
   walking uneven surfaces
   of steep cobblestone streets.

II.
> Rug sellers starting up
> casual conversations,
> giving advice on what
> to do and what to see,
> inviting us to meet
> the family, have apple tea,
> perhaps buy a rug or two
> made by a young woman who
> wove the initials of the boy
> she wanted to marry into the pattern,
> who made a mistake or two
> to prove she is not perfect,
> knows only God can be.

III.

> They swirl the rugs,
> the colors change
> as they settle to earth.

IV.
> Men fish
> shoulder to shoulder
> cover the bridge
> over the Golden Horn,
> fill buckets with water
> from the Bosphorus
> for the fish they catch.
> Below the bridge, restaurant
> maître d's entreat passing
> throngs to fill their bellies,
> the chairs lined up
> like a marching band
> dressed in white shirts.

V.
    Men in prison
    also weave rugs
    for tourists
    to put on unfamiliar floors.

VI.
    Thin women pull
    children along.
    Layers of class
    layers of richness
    forever entwined.
    Istanbul,
    Istanbul,
    Istanbul

section four
RETURN INTO ONE

JO R. DRECHSLER
REDWOOD GROVE

In the Redwood Grove, Spreading Ashes

2007

Thick trunks
and soaring branches
hold sunlit leaves that
shake in the breeze, their
shadows dancing on the ground
travel down the hill with us
to Jo's grove.

Dead leaves and sticks
crunch beneath our feet,
stumps cracked and black
from flames that nourish
the new life that clings
to decaying logs
before the brown
wooden sign.

Jo's ashes will rest
among his beloved Redwoods.

*Big Basin Redwoods State Park
Boulder Creek, California*

Old Growth
2010

I place my hand on the gnarled,
twisted trunk of the old
redwood tree as my son did
on his way to work
at San Jose State University.

He was a skilled craftsman
who taught me new appreciation
for the look, feel, smell,
possibilities, and history
to be found in a piece of wood.

Each day he placed his hand
on the old growth tree,
reverently wrapped arms around
the dark obelisk
laid his head on rough bark,
feeling the toughness of years.

Springing forth from the
black earth a century ago,
just a sapling nurtured by the
virgin soil, empty land waiting
for life to disturb.

He could sense history
in its vibrant,
living warmth,
see a hundred years of
travelers in his mind.

Indian families foraging for food,
Spanish missionaries, bibles packed
in worn saddle bags,
pioneers taking shade from the
blazing California sun.

And finally, those seeking knowledge
who would build a university
around the growing tree,
thousands of students passing by
under its branches.

The strength of years
flowing toward the heavens
straight and tall, reaching toward fresh
morning skies day after day,
year after year.

Until this man came along
on his way to work and stopped,
to place his hand
on the gnarled,
twisted trunk.

Fire in the Bitterroot Valley

2011

Hills topped with
stark tree trunks,
deprived of green clothes
by drunken wildfires
dancing randomly
across the hilltops.

Reduced to domes
of naked sticks
like a bad haircut,
now red foliage
grows underneath,
signaling fall.

Ponderosa pines,
survivors,
huddle in groups,
march up the sides
of brown hills
in fits and starts,
wherever water
is within reach
of thirsty roots.

Just Add Water
Joshua Tree National Park
2010

Sandstone erodes
leaving round rocks
piled high
a giant's playground

Parched life
thorny stems
protection from predators

Tiny leaves
robbing sun rays
of space to dry

Rain, like a magic wand
quenches shriveled throats
of Joshua Trees
staggering across
the sandy desert floor

Scorched, arid shrubs
burst into life
the desert is green

Just add water

Ypres

2009

A lust for power and revenge;
the young pay dearly.

American Memorial Cemetery

Early afternoon drive to Ypres
in a light rain on a gray day.
Enter through a graceful concrete arch
framing a straight grassy path.
Patriotism and love of country
live here,
a slender white cross
soaring skywards
in the distance.

Along the neatly trimmed path,
rounded, pristine white grave stones
rise up in horizontal lines
as far as I can see.
From the earth in front of each stone
red roses, white lilies, yellow daisies,
send up colorful leaves and flowers
that form a soft frame for each name.
The bodies fertilize new beauty and life.

This cemetery is not a place of mourning,
but a celebration of light and spirit.
Names that cannot
be attached to a body are
given a place of honor
on a long, curving
white wall.

German Memorial Cemetery

A narrow opening in a low stone wall.
I gently step onto a
large black granite square.
Red, black and green wreaths
piled high greet me.
26,000 unknown soldiers
rest here, longing
to be remembered
by name.

Raising my eyes higher
to the end of the long path
flanked on either side
by small, black rectangular gravestones
four dark life-size figures,
also nameless,
rise up to meet me.

Rows of three black crosses
randomly spaced
among small dark markers
punctuate the shadows
thrown from the tall trees that shade
the final resting places of so many,
grass trimmed only around the stones.

This was a visit to two WWI cemeteries in Ypres, Belgium.
All the dead from one battle over 4 miles of ground.

I STAND IN FRONT OF A VACANT LOT OVERGROWN GRASS AND WEEDS WAVING BACK AND FORTH

2011

Here I once played in a sand box
    climbed the Japanese Maple tree
    in the back yard

Chased puppies across the lawn

Lay in the sun with my Mom
    slathering baby oil on our reddened skin
    protecting our eyes with pieces of cotton

Hung out sheets on sunny days
    smelling that sweet, clean scent
    as they whipped back and forth
    in Iowa's warm spring winds

Roasted marshmallows over a bonfire
    in the back alley with the neighbor girl
    on cool fall evenings

Made chocolate cokes in the hot summertime

Had slumber parties in the basement
   where we spread sleeping bags
   under the ping pong table

Learned how to twirl a baton
   and turn somersaults and cartwheels

Kissed my boyfriends good night
   on the front porch under the light
   Mom always left on to beckon me
   home

1708 Ellis Boulevard is gone now, swept away by the raging torrent of a moment in Geologic Time in 2008 when a 500 year flood devastated most of my old neighborhood

When God Says No
2014

Week two in France,
Chapel of St. Blaise,
12th century fortifications,
small stone chapel,
golden glow of candles
bathing empty spaces

around the statue,
ropes of smoke
curling upward,
the stark silence
and simplicity of
unadorned walls

she holds her dead son
in her lap, no tears,
only immeasurable sadness
emanating from the
cold gray concrete

that forms the folds
of her clothing
I wonder
if she
asked God

to save her son
as I did
he didn't save his own son
why did I think
he would save mine?

ALONE
2011

I hear the phone
the doctor's voice
it's cancer he says
the world stops

mortality rises up
engulfs me
obliterates comfort
of familiar routine

always another
now my turn
to cross the line
drawn between
well and unwell

no matter how many
surround me
loneliness wraps
my body in its tentacles

I look out
the window,
in the darkness
there is hope

a silver road
rides the night waves
as the moon
shines on

When I Look at My Mother

2009

When I look at my mother
I see myself many years from now.

I see myself in her eyes,
once bright green, now faded.

I see myself in her face,
wrinkled lines, reflecting life.

I see myself in her body,
back bowed from time and gravity.

I see myself in her walk,
a halting, shuffling slide.

I see myself in her smile,
eyes crinkled with love.

I see myself in my mother
many years from now,
and I am afraid.

A Walk on Pebble Beach
2005

Angry white caps toss kelp strands
into the wild blues and greens of the sea
leaving the smell of salt in damp sand.

Gray cliffs jutt out into the water,
breaking relentlessly
into the peacefulness
of white sand beaches.

Seagulls scream into the wind,
waves crash crazily,
all mimicking the landscape
of my brain.

You with less than a year to live
walk by my side
my arm entwined with yours
holds tightly to all I will lose.

I see my reflection looking
back at me as I gaze up at you,
your baldness covered
by a white ball cap.

I wish I could let go
and scream with the gulls.

I Was There to Hear Your Last Breath
2010

Wiping dinner dish
soap from my hands,
I touched your cheek,
heard the last breath
woosh from your lungs
just as I had read about
in a book on death and
what to expect

It's not true your eyes remain open when you die.

We washed your body's
once firm, strong
muscles
ravaged by cancer into
sagging
wrinkled flesh,
disbelief playing a tug of war
with reality as
we struggled to dress you in
long
black pants and shirt
you wore in competitive
mountain bike races

The years of praying, hoping, fighting over,
a guilty sense of relief flows across my brain
images of you drift languidly in front of wet eyes,

walking home from grade school
seeking out the wild asparagus so
I could cook them for dinner,

curled up with Grandma
in your blanket fort
eating chocolate pudding,

the two of us wandering the
lumber stores
you telling me to touch and smell the wood.

I kiss your face to say good-bye.